Overcoming the Odds

Mario Lemieux

Suzanne J. Murdico

RSVP

**RAINTREE
STECK-VAUGHN**
PUBLISHERS
The Steck-Vaughn Company

Austin, Texas

Published by Raintree Steck-Vaughn Publishers,
an imprint of Steck-Vaughn Company

Developed for Steck-Vaughn Company by
Visual Education Corporation, Princeton, New Jersey
Editor: Marilyn Miller
Photo Research: Marty Levick
Electronic Preparation: Cynthia C. Feldner, *Manager;* Christine Osborne
Production Supervisor: Ellen Foos
Electronic Production: Lisa Evans-Skopas, *Manager;*
Elise Dodeles, Deirdre Sheean, Isabelle Verret
Interior Design: Maxson Crandall

Raintree Steck-Vaughn Publishers staff
Editor: Kathy DeVico
Project Manager: Joyce Spicer

Photo Credits: **Cover:** © ALLSPORT; **4:** © Brian Winkler/Bruce Bennett Studios;
7: © AP/Wide World Photos, Inc.; **10:** © Pierre Obendrauf/CANAPRESS Photo Service;
13: © CANAPRESS Photo Service; **15:** © Paul R. Benoit/AP/Wide World Photos, Inc.;
17: © Gary Tramontina/UPI/Bettmann; **18:** © Bill Auth/AP/Wide World Photos, Inc.;
20: © Bruce Bennett Studios; **23:** © ALLSPORT; **26:** © Joyce Mendelsohn/Pittsburgh Post Gazette;
28: © Bob Errey/AP/Wide World Photos, Inc.; **33:** © Paul Hurschmann/AP/Wide World Photos, Inc.;
35: © J. Giamundo/Bruce Bennett Studios; **37:** © Ian Barrett/Reuters/Bettmann;
38: Courtesy of the Pittsburgh Penguins; **42:** © Matt Polk;
43: © Bruce Bennett/Bruce Bennett Studios; **44:** © Gary Hershorn/Reuters/Archive Photos

Library of Congress Cataloging-in-Publication Data
Murdico, Suzanne J.
    Mario Lemieux / Suzanne J. Murdico.
        p.   cm. — (Overcoming the odds)
    Includes bibliographical references (p. 46) and index.
    Summary: Traces the hockey career of the Pittsburgh Penguins star Mario
Lemieux, and discusses the challenge he faced in his battle against Hodgkin's disease.
    ISBN 0-8172-4126-4
    1. Lemieux, Mario, 1965– —Juvenile literature. 2. Hockey players—Canada—
Biography—Juvenile literature. 3. Pittsburgh Penguins (Hockey team)—
Juvenile literature. [1. Lemieux, Mario, 1965– .] I. Title. II. Series.
GV848.5.L46M87 1998
796.962´021—dc21
[B]   97–36691
                                                                                                    CIP
                                                                                                     AC

Printed and bound in the United States
1 2 3 4 5 6 7 8 9 0   WZ   01 00 99 98 97

Table of contents

Chapter 1

The
Comeback Kid

May 11, 1996, was no ordinary Saturday night in Pittsburgh, Pennsylvania. It was game five of the Eastern Conference semifinals of the 1996 Stanley Cup playoffs. The Stanley Cup is the trophy awarded to the best team in the National Hockey League (NHL). In game five, the Pittsburgh Penguins faced the New York Rangers.

In this four-of-seven-game series, the Penguins were leading three games to one. If they won game five, the team would advance to the conference finals. The Penguins would be one step closer to bringing the Stanley Cup home to Pittsburgh for the third time.

The captain of the Penguins was Mario Lemieux. Mario's amazing hockey skills are most often compared with those of the famous Wayne Gretzky, one of hockey's all-time greats.

Mario has one important advantage over Gretzky, though. At 6 feet and 170 pounds, Gretzky is smaller

Mario led the Pittsburgh Penguins to victory over the New York Rangers in the semifinals of the 1996 Stanley Cup playoffs.

and thinner than Mario, who is 6 feet 4 inches tall and weighs 220 pounds. Mario uses his size and strength to shield the puck from opposing teams.

"You just try to keep yourself between Mario and your net," explains New York Ranger Mark Messier.

Halfway through the first period of game five, Mario scored the first goal for the Penguins. Shortly into the second period, his teammate Jaromir Jagr shot the puck into the net. The score was 2–0. Then it was the Rangers' turn to score, but Mario responded quickly with a third goal for the Penguins.

The Rangers rallied with back-to-back goals to tie the score at 3–3. Not to be outdone, Jagr scored back-to-back goals of his own. This put the Penguins in the lead by two points late in the second period.

Bryan Smolinski of the Penguins added another goal to make the score 6–3. Now Mario went to work once again. He scored another goal to complete a hat trick. A hat trick means that one player scores three goals in the same game. After Mario scored his hat trick, the Pittsburgh fans threw a flurry of hats down onto the ice.

When the game ended, the Pittsburgh Penguins had beaten the New York Rangers by a score of 7–3. The team now advanced to the conference finals.

The *New York Times* compared Mario with basketball superstar Michael Jordan. "Whatever His Airness does in sneakers," the paper said, "Lemieux does on skates."

Mario follows Jaromir Jagr onto the ice.

The victory was especially sweet for Mario. It came after years of health problems that had threatened both his career and his life. It came after a year-long absence from the game. It came after many people, sometimes including even Mario himself, had thought that he might never be able to play hockey again. But once more Mario Lemieux overcame overwhelming odds to return to the sport that he was born to play.

Chapter 2

A Born Skater

Mario Lemieux was born in Montreal, Quebec, on October 5, 1965. Quebec is a province in Canada, the large country that is north of the United States. Mario is the youngest of three boys. His father, Jean-Guy, was a construction worker. Mario's mother, Pierrette, was a homemaker.

Most people in Canada speak English. In Quebec, however, most people are French-Canadian. They speak and write in French. The Lemieux family is French-Canadian. So Mario grew up speaking French, not English.

In Canada, ice hockey is the national sport. The people who live in Montreal are especially great fans of hockey. Many young boys there are encouraged to ice-skate and to play hockey almost as soon as they can walk. "Growing up in Montreal, you want to be a hockey player," Mario recalled. "You see the Montreal Canadiens win all those Stanley Cups. My goal was to do that one year."

Mario started playing hockey when he was only three years old. His older brothers, Alain and Richard, had already been playing for several years. Mr. and Mrs. Lemieux said that they sometimes made their own rink for indoor practice. They packed snow in the hallway inside the house.

"The boys were so young that they were skating more on the boots than on the blades, but it was fun," Mario's mother remembered.

The boys also spent many hours practicing on the rink across the street from their house. By the age of six, Mario was playing hockey on a team with other boys his age. The team was called the Ville Emard Hurricanes, and Mario played center. The center is an offensive position. Mario's main responsibility as center was to score goals and to pass the puck to his teammates so that they could score goals.

Mario's brothers also continued to play in Canadian junior amateur hockey leagues. Mario even wore the same jersey—number 27—as his brother Alain. It was Mario, though, who was noticed for his talent on the ice. He led the Hurricanes to many team championships while also winning individual scoring titles.

Mario always wanted to win, and he usually did. His competitive nature was also evident off the ice. Even when Mario was playing cards or a board game, he did not like to lose. "If Mario lost, it would be like a hurricane went through the basement," his father said.

In 1981, when he was 16, Mario began playing in the Quebec Major Junior Hockey League (QMJHL).

He was chosen by a team called the Laval Voisins. Although this was still amateur hockey, he was paid a small amount—$35 a week—for expenses. By this time Mario had not only become a very skillful hockey player but had also grown into a large teenager. He now stood 6 feet 4 inches tall and weighed 200 pounds.

Mario's size gave him an advantage over other players. His long reach allowed him to steal the puck and keep it away from the other team. Mario's large physical presence also made goalies nervous.

At this time Mario decided to change the number on his jersey. He thought about taking number 99—in honor of Wayne Gretzky. Many people consider Gretzky the greatest player in the history of the NHL. But Mario decided that he shouldn't wear the same number as his idol. Instead, he chose to wear 66, which is 99 upside down.

The town of Laval was not far from the Lemieux home. This was an advantage for Mario, who was

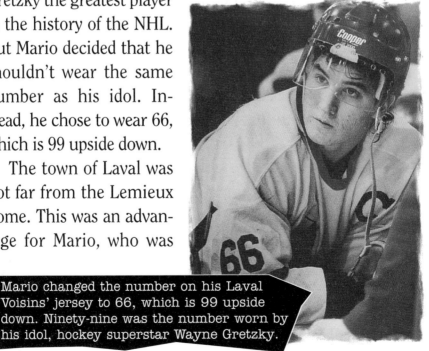

Mario changed the number on his Laval Voisins' jersey to 66, which is 99 upside down. Ninety-nine was the number worn by his idol, hockey superstar Wayne Gretzky.

very close to his family. Because of the Voisins' schedule, though, Mario often stayed at a Laval boarding-house rather than at his family's home.

Mario played well during his first season with Laval. He scored 30 goals and had 66 assists. But many people had very high expectations for Mario. Some of them were disappointed by his rookie, or first-year, performance.

Before the start of his second season, Mario made an important decision. He decided to quit school and concentrate only on hockey. "I wanted to be able to skate in the morning and play hockey at night without being tired for the game," Mario said. "I figured I could do my learning through living and traveling."

Mr. and Mrs. Lemieux would have liked Mario to finish school. They knew, though, that their son had a rare talent. Eventually, they agreed that Mario should focus just on that talent.

In his second season in the junior league, Mario's performance improved dramatically. He scored 84 goals and assisted on 100 other goals. Mario's third season was even better. He set new league records with 133 goals and 149 assists—an amazing total of 282 points in only 70 games! In hockey, goals and assists are worth equal points in contributing to each player's statistics.

Now Mario was living up to everyone's expectations. No one doubted that he was the best player in the junior league. He was ready for the majors.

Chapter 3

A Rising Star

Every team in the NHL wanted 18-year-old Mario Lemieux. According to NHL rules, however, the team with the worst record is given the first draft choice. That team was the Pittsburgh Penguins.

The Penguins had had a poor record for many years. In fact, some people thought that the team might be moved to a different city.

In 1984, though, the Pittsburgh Penguins chose Mario Lemieux to join the team. "No one who's come out of junior hockey has ever shown as much potential as Mario—ever," said Bob Berry, the Penguins' coach.

The Penguins gave Mario the highest rookie salary in the history of the NHL. He would receive $350,000 per season for his first two years with the team. Mario also made sure that his parents would receive a satellite dish for their home in Canada. That way the family could watch the Penguins' games on television.

The Penguins knew that it would be difficult for Mario to adjust to his new life. He was still a teenager. He would be living in a new country, and he spoke

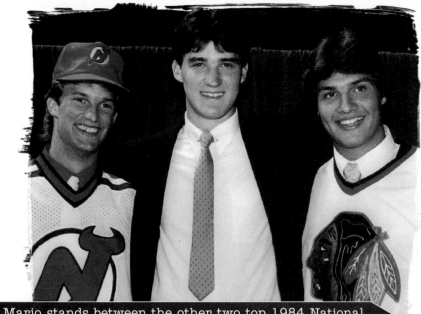

Mario stands between the other two top 1984 National Hockey League draft picks. On his right is Kirk Muller, who was selected by the New Jersey Devils, and on his left is Ed Olczyk, who was chosen by the Chicago Blackhawks.

very little English. So the team arranged to have Mario live with a family in the Pittsburgh area.

Mario moved into the home of Tom and Nancy Mathews. The Mathewses had three sons who were around Mario's age. Mario and the Mathews family got along well. Even after Mario became a star player, he still found time to play street hockey with the Mathews boys. And Mario said that Nancy Mathews was like a second mother to him. Later on, when Mario moved into his own apartment, he chose a place that was not far from the Mathewses' home.

Living with the Mathewses was good for Mario. Even so, he had some trouble adjusting to his new life and surroundings. "He was very quiet and very shy," said Nancy Mathews. "The language problem was very difficult for him."

Although Mario had taken English lessons while he was still in Canada, he did not speak the language well. He found it difficult to communicate, especially with reporters. "I used to run into the bathroom after games so I wouldn't have to talk to reporters," he said.

During his first year in the United States, Mario found a unique way to teach himself English. "I watched a lot of soap operas on television," he explained later.

Mario was under a great deal of pressure to improve the Penguins' performance. Before he joined the team, the Pittsburgh stadium was often more than half empty when the Penguins played.

After Mario came to Pittsburgh, that situation began to turn around. Attendance at home games rose from about 6,800 people to more than 10,000.

Paul Steigerwald, the Penguins' director of marketing, gave all the credit for the increase in attendance to Mario. "Without him, the team doesn't improve, and the fans don't come out."

Mario did not disappoint his team or his fans. In his first game with the Penguins, he scored a goal. By April, at the end of his first season, Mario had scored 43 goals and made 57 assists for a total of 100 points. That was the third-highest point total earned by a rookie. Only two players—Peter Stastny (1981)

Mario reacts joyously after scoring his first NHL goal. It was against the Boston Bruins on October 11, 1984.

and Dale Hawerchuk (1982)—scored more in their first seasons. Mario was so impressive that he was named the NHL's Rookie of the Year.

Even with Mario's great talent, the Penguins ended the season with a 24–51–5 record. It was the worst record in the division and the second worst in the league. As in any team sport, a single player can't do it all. The Penguins needed other skilled players who could work with Mario.

After the 1984–1985 season, Mario participated in the All-Star Game held in Canada. During this game, he played against the brightest stars in the NHL. His team, the Wales Conference, won the game. Mario was named the Most Valuable Player (MVP). For that honor he won a four-wheel-drive car, which he generously gave to his brother Richard. "It was a great feeling to play in the All-Star Game my first year in the league," Mario said.

Mario continued to play well during his second season in Pittsburgh. He had 48 goals and 93 assists for a total of 141 points. Only Wayne Gretzky scored more during the season. That season Gretzky had broken the NHL scoring record with an amazing 215 points. Although Gretzky took the scoring title, the league's players chose Mario as the most outstanding player in the NHL. For that achievement he received the Lester B. Pearson Award.

During that 1985–1986 season, the Penguins began to show improvement. They finished with a 34–38–8 record, their best since 1978–1979. The team still ended up in fifth place, however, and did not make it into the Stanley Cup playoffs.

Even so, the Pittsburgh fans finally had a team to cheer about. Eddie Johnston, the general manager, said, "Mario means at least a point and a half or two points a game for us. When he's out there, he upgrades the skills of everybody else."

To keep their star, the Penguins signed a new contract with Mario. Over the next five seasons, he would earn $2.75 million, the second-highest salary in hockey. Only Wayne Gretzky earned more.

Mario celebrates with his mother after signing a new five-year contract with the Penguins in 1986. Only Wayne Gretzky of the Edmonton Oilers was paid more.

Although he missed 17 games during the 1986–1987 season because of injuries, Mario still scored 54 goals and had 53 assists for a total of 107 points. Once again Gretzky took the scoring title with 183 points. And once again the Penguins did not make the playoffs.

Just before the start of the next season, Mario and some top hockey players from Canadian teams were selected to represent their country in the Canada Cup. In this tournament they played against other all-star teams (each made up of the participating country's best hockey players) from around the world. For the first time, Mario was on the same team as Wayne

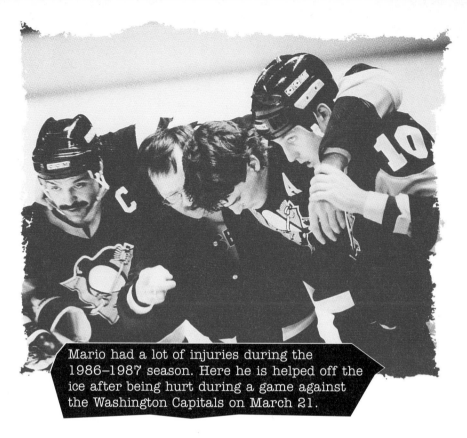

Mario had a lot of injuries during the 1986–1987 season. Here he is helped off the ice after being hurt during a game against the Washington Capitals on March 21.

Gretzky. "Every shift, every time we were on the ice, Wayne tried to do the impossible," Mario said.

Gretzky had compliments for Mario, too. "We think the same things, go to the same holes, see everything the same way," he said.

With Mario and Gretzky leading the way, Team Canada won the Canada Cup in 1987. Mario scored 11 goals, more than any other player in the tournament. Nine of those goals, including the tournament-winning goal, were from passes by Gretzky.

"Playing alongside Wayne gave me a lot of confidence in myself," Mario said. "And I brought it back to Pittsburgh."

Chapter 4

Pittsburgh's Finest

Before the 1987–1988 hockey season, Wayne Gretzky had dominated the NHL awards. For seven years in a row, he had won the Art Ross Trophy. That meant that he was the NHL's leading scorer. For eight years in a row, Gretzky had also won the Hart Trophy. That award is given to the most valuable player of the regular season.

But in 1988 all that changed. Mario Lemieux finally broke Gretzky's incredible winning streak. He had 70 goals and 98 assists during the season. With this total of 168 points, Mario beat out the Great One for the scoring title. Gretzky had 40 goals and 109 assists for a second-place total of 149 points. Mario won the Art Ross Trophy and the Hart Trophy.

There was no question that Mario was challenging Gretzky as the greatest player. Mario was now a celebrity, and younger fans looked up to him. He wanted to be a good role model, as Gretzky was.

With Mario's help, the Penguins were a winning team. They finished the 1987–1988 season with a 36–35–9 record. The Penguins thought that they

Mario received two of hockey's biggest trophies for his play in 1987–1988—the Hart Trophy (left) and the Art Ross Trophy (right).

were finally going to qualify for the Stanley Cup playoffs. But on the final day of the season, the New Jersey Devils clinched the last playoff spot in the division.

Although the Penguins failed to make the playoffs, they had started to acquire talented players who could support Mario. These players included goaltender Tom Barrasso, defenseman Paul Coffey, and right wing Rob Brown.

For the 1988–1989 season, Mario was named captain of the Penguins. It was the beginning of a great year for Mario. Hockey is traditionally a low-scoring game. But during one game in October, Mario made an incredible eight points. Such a feat had been seen only 11 times in the history of the NHL.

In most hockey games, the total score earned by both teams is less than eight points. So it is an extraordinary achievement when a single player has eight in one game.

Then, on New Year's Eve, Mario did the incredible again. In a game against the New Jersey Devils, he made another eight points! Mario and Gretzky are the only two players to have done this twice in a season.

During that game on New Year's Eve, Mario did something else that has never happened before or since in the NHL. He scored goals in five different ways. He scored one goal when both teams were even—five skaters on each side.

Mario scored another goal during a Penguin power play. In a power play one team has one more player on the ice than the other team does. This happens when a player on the opposing team is in the penalty box for a certain period of time. Penalties are given for such offenses as holding the puck, tripping another player, and fighting. Mario scored a third goal during a Devil power play when one Penguin player was in the penalty box for a foul.

Mario's fourth goal came on a penalty shot. This means that Mario had a free shot against the goalie, in which he was allowed to skate by himself. Mario shot his final goal into an empty net. The Devils had removed their goaltender so that they could have an extra skater on the ice.

Penguin Rob Brown was deeply impressed by his teammate. "It was a classic example of the best hockey player in the world," he said.

Mario ended the season with 85 goals and 114 assists. This 199-point total earned him the league scoring title for the second year in a row. And for the first time since Mario came to Pittsburgh, the Penguins were one of the four teams from each division that made it into the Stanley Cup playoffs. These eight teams had the best winning records in their divisions.

The playoff series started out well for Mario and the Penguins. They beat the New York Rangers in four straight games. In the next round, the Penguins faced the Philadelphia Flyers. The series was tied at two games each. During the fifth game, Mario did the amazing yet again. With five goals and three assists, he had another eight-point game!

With this win the Penguins had a 3–2 lead over Philadelphia. But then the Flyers came back and won the next two games. The Penguins were now out of the Stanley Cup contest. Mario was disappointed, but he was determined to come back the next year. "I know I'll drink from that cup one day," Mario said. "I just know it."

Even though they didn't win the Stanley Cup, the Penguins were very happy with their star player. The team's management gave Mario a new five-year contract worth $10 million plus bonuses.

The 1989–1990 season started slowly for Mario and the Penguins. They were not playing as well as they had been, and Mario was trailing Gretzky in scoring.

But soon the Penguins became a winning team again. In November Mario began putting together a hot scoring streak. Before it was over, he had passed Gretzky in the scoring race. Many people thought that Mario could even beat Gretzky's scoring-streak record of 51 consecutive games.

Just as things were looking up for the team, Mario noticed that he had severe back pain that would not

Mario put together a hot scoring streak during the 1989–1990 season.

go away. Doctors told him that he had a damaged disk in his spinal column. He would probably need to have surgery to fix it. Afterward, they weren't sure if he would ever be able to play hockey again!

But Mario had the true champion's courage. He wore a back brace and continued to play, although his injury was still incredibly painful. Sometimes he couldn't even bend over to lace his own skates.

In February even Mario could no longer stand the pain. His scoring streak ended. Still, it was astonishing that he had either earned a goal or made an assist for 46 games in a row.

Mario could not play for the rest of the year. At the end of the season, he did participate in one more game and earned three points. It was not enough, though. Without their star player, the Penguins failed to win a place in the Stanley Cup playoffs.

In July 1990 Mario had surgery. Doctors removed the damaged part of the disk from his back. Mario hoped to recover in time to return to the ice for the start of the new season. By October he was skating again. But soon the pain in his back returned—worse than before.

Now his doctors found that Mario had developed an infection in his back. To recover, he would need to take medicine and rest for at least three months. That meant missing two-thirds of the hockey season. Some hockey insiders wondered if Mario would ever feel well enough to return to hockey.

Chapter 5

The Road to the Stanley Cup

The Pittsburgh Penguins began the 1990–1991 season without Mario. Over the years, though, they had acquired several talented players. The Penguins had grown into a strong team, and they were playing very well.

Meanwhile Mario spent most of his time in bed, resting and recuperating. It was tremendously frustrating. Mario wanted to be on the ice, helping his teammates. But he understood that he needed to feel well again before he could play his best.

At the end of December, his doctors finally allowed Mario to begin exercising. He started riding on a stationary bicycle to build up his strength. After a few weeks, he was feeling stronger, and the doctors agreed to let him back on the ice. By the end of January, he was once again playing hockey with the Penguins.

Mario played in the final 26 games of the regular season. Even though he played in so few games, he had 19 goals and 26 assists. He helped the Penguins finish the season with a 41–33–6 record. They took

Reporters watch as Mario exercises on his stationary bike to help him regain his strength after back surgery.

first place in their division and earned a spot in the Stanley Cup playoffs.

In the first round of the playoffs, the Penguins beat the New Jersey Devils. Then they faced the Washington Capitals in their division finals. After being tied with the Capitals at one game apiece, the Penguins took the next three games to win the series.

In the conference finals, the Penguins met the Boston Bruins. The Bruins took the first two games. But the Penguins were a determined team, and they came back to win the next four games in a row. The Penguins now advanced to the Stanley Cup finals against the Minnesota North Stars.

Pittsburgh lost the first game to Minnesota but came back to win the second. Then, before game three, Mario was sidelined with back spasms, and the Penguins lost. Mario returned to the ice for game four, and he helped his team to win. The Penguins went on to win the fifth game as well. Now they were only one victory away from the Stanley Cup.

In the sixth game, the Penguins dominated the ice from the beginning. They scored three goals to none in the first period. After that the North Stars never had a chance. The Pittsburgh Penguins shut out their opponents with a score of 8–0. Mario and his teammates had finally won the Stanley Cup!

As the captain of the winning team, Mario was presented with the Stanley Cup. As is the tradition, he held the cup over his head and skated around the ice rink. "It was no strain on my back to lift it," Mario joked later. He was surrounded by his teammates, and they passed the cup back and forth so that each player had a turn with it.

During the playoffs Mario had scored 16 goals and 28 assists for a 44-point total. Only one player— Wayne Gretzky—had ever scored more points in the playoffs. Gretzky's record of 47 points was set in 1985. Mario won the 1991 Conn Smythe Trophy, one of hockey's most highly regarded awards, as Most Valuable Player.

Mario's teammates recognized how important Mario's contribution was to the team's Stanley Cup

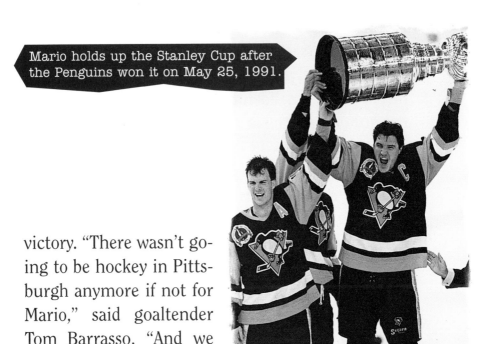

victory. "There wasn't going to be hockey in Pittsburgh anymore if not for Mario," said goaltender Tom Barrasso. "And we wouldn't have won the cup without him."

Mario, in turn, praised the Penguins' coach, Bob Johnson. "Nobody thought we could win the cup," Mario said. "But Bob came here and was so positive. He made us believe anything was possible. He convinced us we could win the Stanley Cup."

Coach Johnson became ill before the start of the 1991–1992 hockey season. Doctors found that he had brain cancer. Bob Johnson died in November 1991.

"Bob was a great teacher," recalled Mario sadly. "And more than anything else, he taught us how to win."

During the 1991–1992 season, Mario was still bothered by back pain and missed a few games. Even so, he finished the season with 44 goals and 87 assists for 131 points. This total exceeded Gretzky's and earned Mario the scoring title.

The Penguins didn't have a great year, but they did make it into the Stanley Cup playoffs. Not everyone believed that the team had what it took to win the championship again. "When you win once, people wonder," explained Kevin Stevens, the Penguins' forward. "When you win twice, it's no fluke." The Penguins were determined to prove that their Stanley Cup victory was no fluke.

It wouldn't be easy, though. In the first round, they were nearly eliminated by the Washington Capitals. The series went to seven games, but the Penguins eventually won. Their next opponents were the New York Rangers. Pittsburgh won the first game. In the heat of game two, the Rangers' Adam Graves slashed Mario with his stick, breaking a bone in Mario's hand. As a result, Mario had to sit out the rest of the series.

Pittsburgh went on to beat the Rangers, even without Mario. In the conference finals, the Penguins faced the Boston Bruins. Mario returned to the ice in the second game. Incredibly, even though his broken hand had not yet healed, he scored two goals and an assist. He helped his team win the series in four straight games. The Penguins now advanced to the Stanley Cup finals.

Their challengers were the Chicago Blackhawks. In game one, the Blackhawks took a 4–1 lead. But the Penguins rallied to trail them by just one point.

Then a young 20-year-old Penguin named Jaromir Jagr made an impressive goal to tie the score. Next, with 13 seconds remaining, Mario scored the winning goal.

The Blackhawks were never able to regain control. The Penguins won the Stanley Cup finals in four straight games. They brought the cup back to Pittsburgh for the second year in a row. And once again Mario was awarded the Conn Smythe Trophy as playoff MVP.

Blackhawks' coach Mike Keenan said, "We were just beaten by a better club. They have youth, experience, and the greatest player in the world."

By this time Mario's hockey skills had become legendary. A reporter for *Sports Illustrated* wrote, "He shoots with deadly accuracy and passes with precision. His reach is simply superhuman, and he has an uncanny knack for deception."

When Mario has the puck, opposing goalies become scared. "You know you can't stop him," says Tim Cheveldae, goalie for the Detroit Red Wings. "You just hope to contain him. He'll do anything to keep you off balance. And you know what? It works."

Mario, naturally, doesn't feel bad about the fear he arouses in opposing players. "I have no sympathy for goalies," he says with a smile. "My job is to go out there and score goals, and their job is to try and stop me." And Mario did his job better than just about anyone.

Chapter 6

Tragedy and Triumph

The 1992–1993 season started as one of the best for both Mario and the Penguins. Mario had signed a seven-year contract with the team. He was guaranteed $6 million per year. Mario showed that he was worth it by going on a scoring spree. Halfway through the season, he had earned 104 points. It looked as if he was on his way to breaking Gretzky's 215-point record.

But then something happened that would change everything. Mario's career—as well as his life—was about to be seriously threatened.

In January 1993 Mario was not feeling well. He had a sore throat, and the pain in his back had returned. Mario also had a lump on his neck. He had first felt the lump about a year and a half earlier. But he thought it was nothing, so he had never mentioned it to a doctor—until now.

The doctor decided to operate on Mario to remove the lump. When doctors examined the lump, they found out that Mario was very sick. He had Hodgkin's disease, a form of cancer. Hodgkin's disease affects the lymph nodes, which are part of the body's immune system. The immune system helps the body resist infection.

When the doctor told Mario what was wrong, he was very upset. "I could hardly drive home because of the tears," he said. "I was crying all day." Mario wanted to tell his longtime girlfriend, Nathalie Asselin, but he could hardly speak. After almost an hour, he was finally able to explain why he was so upset.

There was some good news. The cancer had been caught early. Doctors told Mario that he had a 90 to 95 percent chance of being cured. Those were very good odds.

A few days after Mario found out about his illness, he called a press conference. He would have to take time off from playing hockey, and he wanted to let people know why. By this time Mario had overcome his initial shock and sadness. He was now ready to confront the disease openly and fight back.

"I've faced a lot of battles since I was really young, and I've always come out on top," he told reporters. "I expect that will be the case with this disease."

Mario was showing great bravery and honesty. After all, he knew that cancer was very serious. One of Mario's cousins had died from Hodgkin's disease. Two of Mario's uncles had died from other types of cancer. And the Penguins' coach, Bob Johnson, had died of brain cancer.

After his cancer was discovered in 1993, Mario spoke openly about his health to the press.

Even so, Mario Lemieux is a fighter. He wanted to recover not only for himself but also for his team. "I'll be back when I'm 100 percent cured," he said.

The first thing was to rid his body of the cancer. Mario needed to have radiation treatment. If any cancer cells were in Mario's body, the radiation would kill them.

Receiving radiation treatment is similar to having X rays taken, but the rays are 50 times stronger. People who are treated with radiation often feel very tired and weak. Afterward they usually need a great deal of rest before they feel better.

Five days a week for five weeks, Mario received radiation treatments. He had his final treatment on

March 2, 1993. That night the Penguins were playing a game against the Philadelphia Flyers. Mario boarded a plane and flew to Philadelphia to help his teammates.

When Mario skated onto the ice, the people of Philadelphia did something unusual. Even though Mario was a member of the opposing team, they gave him a standing ovation! Everyone knew that Mario had been sick, and they were happy to see this great player back on the ice. They also knew that Mario was doing something extraordinary. Most people would have spent several weeks resting after radiation treatment. But Mario Lemieux is not most people, and his doctor had told him to do what he could when he felt ready.

His doctor had thought that Mario would last only a few minutes on the ice. But he stayed in the game for 20 minutes. Mario scored one goal and assisted on another! He had once again lived up to his nickname, "Mario the Magnificent."

Mario's cancer was in remission. That means that his doctors found no more signs of it. But Mario still needed to have regular checkups and tests to make sure that the cancer did not return.

Before he became sick, Mario had been leading the league in scoring for the 1992–1993 season. While he was recovering, however, Pat LaFontaine of the Buffalo Sabres had taken a 12-point lead over Mario. "I thought about it even during radiation," he said later. "I was determined to come back and regain the lead."

And that is what Mario did. For the rest of the season, he played great hockey. Although he was worn out from the radiation, Mario scored goal after goal. In fact, he scored five goals in one game against the New York Rangers!

Even after missing 23 games during the season, Mario still won his fourth scoring title. He had 69 goals and 91 assists for a total of 160 points. Mario had fought against overwhelming odds—and won.

At the same time, Mario had led the Pittsburgh Penguins to the best regular-season record in the league. The team had high hopes of winning a third straight Stanley Cup.

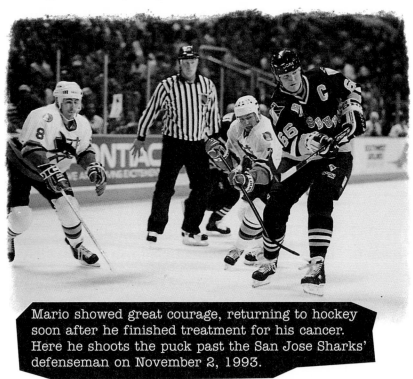

Mario showed great courage, returning to hockey soon after he finished treatment for his cancer. Here he shoots the puck past the San Jose Sharks' defenseman on November 2, 1993.

In the first round of the playoffs, the Penguins faced the New Jersey Devils. Mario played well and led his team to victory in five games.

The Penguins' rivals in the next round were the New York Islanders. Unfortunately, Mario was sidelined with back spasms for part or all of several games in the series.

The teams were tied at three games each, so the series went to a seventh game. In the final minutes of that game, the Penguins tied the score. Much to the team's disappointment, though, the Islanders won the game in overtime. The Pittsburgh Penguins would not take home a third Stanley Cup.

But Mario had several significant individual achievements. Not only did he receive the Art Ross Trophy as the season's highest scorer, but he was also awarded his second Hart Trophy as league MVP. In addition, he won his third Lester B. Pearson Award as players' choice of MVP. And for his perseverance, sportsmanship, and dedication to hockey, he was presented with the Masterton Trophy.

Mario had other happy moments in 1993. In June he married Nathalie Asselin in the couple's hometown of Montreal. That same year Mario and Nathalie also became the proud parents of their first child—a daughter named Lauren Rachel.

After having survived cancer, Mario formed the Mario Lemieux Foundation to support cancer research. Although Mario is a very private person, he

Mario and his bride leave the church after their June 1993 wedding.

always makes time for fans who need his help. "If someone wants me to talk to a sick kid or a sick family member," he says, "it's something I want to do."

Although Mario's cancer was in remission, he continued to suffer from back pain. Over the summer, he had another operation on his back. But the pain was so severe that he played in only 22 games during the 1993–1994 season. The Penguins did not have a great season either. They earned a spot in the Stanley Cup playoffs but lost in the first round.

It seemed as if Mario might not be well enough to play hockey anymore. He often felt tired, and he

Even before his illness, Mario was ready with a helping hand. One program he has participated in outfits children with $100 worth of clothing.

lacked his former strength. At the end of the season, Mario said that he was thinking about retiring.

Later, doctors determined that Mario had a medical condition called anemia. This condition, which is not life threatening, can cause a person to feel tired. Mario had probably developed anemia as a result of the radiation treatments he received.

Ultimately, Mario decided not to retire. He did, however, decide to sit out the 1994–1995 season. "I need to regain the strength I had two years ago," Mario said. "I get tired very quickly."

Questions remained, though. Would Mario ever fully recover and be able to play hockey again? Even if he did come back, would he be the great hockey star he had once been?

Chapter 7

Back on the Ice

THE THREE MOST FEARED WORDS IN HOCKEY—MARIO IS BACK. This is how Pittsburgh advertised the fact that its star player, Mario Lemieux, had rejoined the Penguins for the 1995–1996 season.

It was impossible to tell that Mario had been away from hockey for 18 months. In his first game back, he assisted on four goals to help his team beat the Toronto Maple Leafs. The game was played in Pittsburgh, and the hometown fans went wild.

"He could have said goodbye, but he wanted to come back, to play," said Mario's teammate Ron Francis. "That's what makes the great players great—they absolutely love the game."

The world was glad not only that Mario was playing hockey again but, more importantly, that he was healthy. Much of the reason for his good health was a new training routine. Mario had spent many months working out with a personal trainer. He was running on a treadmill, riding a stationary bicycle, and lifting weights. These workouts helped strengthen his back so that he could play hockey without pain.

Mario also seemed to be having fun on the ice. "If you have a second chance to do something you love, you appreciate it more," he says. "Sometimes you take it for granted, but when you miss it for a year and are able to come back, you feel different."

Although Mario was fit and happy to be playing hockey, he wanted to conserve his energy and avoid any more back problems. So at the beginning of the season, Mario announced that he would play in 60 to 70 games. He decided to skip the second of back-to-back games. He also would not travel to all of the games on the West Coast.

By November, Mario felt so good that he was even playing in back-to-back games. Toward the end of the regular season, the Penguins had the best record in their division. "The number one reason for us being in first place is because of 66," said Eddie Johnston, the Penguins' coach.

Because he was playing so well, few knew that Mario was having a rough time off the ice. He and his wife were expecting their third child. The doctors ordered her to stay in bed for several months to ensure a safe delivery. When he wasn't playing, Mario was by her side constantly. Said Coach Johnston, "I don't know where he gets the strength, but he was able to play through stuff like that."

Mario and Nathalie's son, Austin Nicholas, was born in March. Although Nathalie gave birth three months early, both mother and baby were fine.

Nothing, it seemed, stopped Mario—either personally or professionally. Even after being away from hockey for so long, he had not lost any of his great skill.

The goaltenders in the NHL could attest to that. When asked which player they most feared when he was skating toward them with a puck, more than half of the goalies named Mario. Kirk McLean, goalie for the Vancouver Canucks, explained why: "He's a big man with speed, he's shifty, and he's got a long reach."

It's not surprising that goalies start to worry when they see Mario coming. For the 1995–1996 season, he once again led the league, scoring 161 points. For this accomplishment he won his fifth Art Ross Trophy. Mario wasn't finished yet, though. "Winning the scoring title was satisfying personally, but I came back to win another championship in Pittsburgh," he said.

Unfortunately for Mario and his teammates, the Stanley Cup did not return to Pittsburgh. The Penguins took the first round against the Washington Capitals and the second round against the New York Rangers. But the winning stopped there. In the third round, the Florida Panthers beat the Penguins, knocking them out of the Stanley Cup playoffs.

Despite this loss, Mario had another unbelievable season. Simply being able to play hockey again at such a high level was an incredible achievement. Even Mario's opponents were awed. "Mario has taken 'comeback' to a different realm," said Kevin Lowe, a player for the New York Rangers.

Besides the Art Ross Trophy, Mario added other awards to his collection. He won his third Hart Trophy and his fourth Lester B. Pearson Award.

Although hockey is a major part of Mario's life, his family is also very important to him. He gives a lot of credit to his wife, Nathalie, for helping him through his illnesses. "With the back infection, she was my nurse for three months," he says. "She was there every day." Mario and Nathalie own a large house with five fireplaces. Their home is in Sewickley, Pennsylvania, near Pittsburgh. They live there with their three children—Lauren, Stephanie, and Austin.

Off the ice, Mario is polite, kind, and soft-spoken. He enjoys being at home with his family. Mario also

Mario poses with his daughter Lauren and the family dogs in front of their home in Pennsylvania.

Mario's love of golf enables him to help others by hosting a yearly golf tournament to aid cancer research.

loves to play golf. "His idea of a perfect summer day," says former teammate Rick Tocchet, "is to play golf with a few friends and then go home to his family for a quiet dinner."

It seems that Mario is very talented at golf, too. Mario even combines his love of golf with helping others. Every year he hosts a golf tournament that benefits cancer research.

At the end of the 1995–1996 hockey season, Mario talked again about retirement. No one would have been surprised if he had decided to end his hockey career. He had suffered through many serious health problems. But he had come back, time and time again.

Mario decided to return for the 1996–1997 season. He wanted to finish his career with a third Stanley

Cup for the Penguins. But the team did not accomplish that feat. The Penguins were defeated in the first round of the playoffs by the Philadelphia Flyers.

Earlier in the season, Mario had announced that he would definitely retire after the playoffs. Although his team didn't win another Stanley Cup, Mario took home his sixth Art Ross Trophy as scoring leader. When Mario Lemieux retired from hockey in 1997, he was still the best in the game. After all, that's what *le mieux* means in French—"the best."

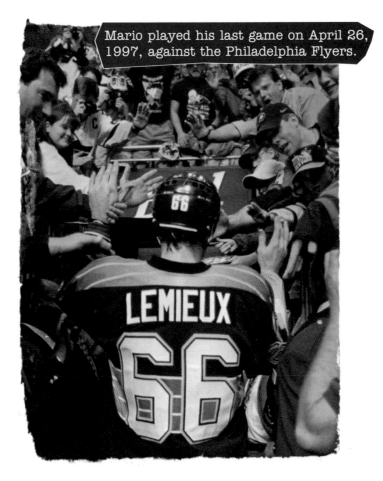

Mario played his last game on April 26, 1997, against the Philadelphia Flyers.

Mario Lemieux's
Career Highlights

1984   Selected as number one draft choice of Pittsburgh Penguins.

1985   Named All-Star Game's Most Valuable Player.
Awarded Calder Memorial Trophy as NHL's Rookie of the Year.

1986   Won Lester B. Pearson Award for outstanding player, by vote of members of the NHL.

1987   With Wayne Gretzky, led Team Canada to win the Canada Cup.

1988   Won Art Ross Trophy as scoring leader.
Awarded Hart Trophy as NHL's Most Valuable Player.
Won second Lester B. Pearson Award.

1989   Won second Art Ross Trophy.
Named Player of the Year by the *Sporting News*.

1991   Led Pittsburgh Penguins to Stanley Cup victory.
Won Conn Smythe Trophy as playoff's Most Valuable Player.

1992   Won third Art Ross Trophy.
Led Pittsburgh Penguins to second straight Stanley Cup victory.
Won second Conn Smythe Trophy.

1993   After diagnosis and treatment of Hodgkin's disease, returned to hockey in March and led Penguins into Stanley Cup playoffs.
Won fourth Art Ross Trophy as scoring leader, even after missing 23 games.
Awarded second Hart Trophy.
Won third Lester B. Pearson Award.
Received Masterton Trophy for perseverance, sportsmanship, and dedication.

1994   Sat out 1994–1995 season to recover from Hodgkin's disease, anemia, and back problems.

1995   Returned to hockey and led Penguins into Stanley Cup playoffs.

1996   Won fifth Art Ross Trophy.
Awarded third Hart Trophy.
Won fourth Lester B. Pearson Award.

1997   Won sixth Art Ross Trophy.
Announced retirement at the end of the 1996–1997 season.

Further Reading

Ayers, Tom. *The Illustrated Rules of Ice Hockey.* Nashville, TN: Ideals Children's Books, 1995.

Cox, Ted. *Mario Lemieux: Super Mario.* Chicago: Children's Press, 1993.

Gutman, Bill. *Ice Hockey: Start Right and Play Well.* Freeport, NY: Marshall Cavendish, 1990.

———. *Mario Lemieux: Wizard with a Puck.* Brookfield, CT: Millbrook, 1992.

Harris, Lisa. *Hockey.* Austin, TX: Raintree Steck-Vaughn, 1994.

Jensen, Julie. *Beginning Hockey.* Minneapolis, MN: Lerner, 1996.

Klein, Jeff Z. *Mario Lemieux: Ice Hockey Star.* New York: Chelsea House, 1995.

Knapp, Ron. *Sports Great Mario Lemieux.* Springfield, NJ: Enslow, 1995.

Index

Index *cont.*